AF887598

ANDREW G.
NELSON

UNCOMMON VALOR II

Challenge Coins of the NYPD Emergency Service Unit

ANDREW G. NELSON

UNCOMMON VALOR II – Challenge Coins of the NYPD Emergency Service Unit

Published by Huntzman Enterprises

HUNTZMAN ENTERPRISES

First Edition: February 2017

ISBN-10: 0-9987562-1-0

ISBN-13: 978-0-9987562-1-9

Printed in the United States of America

1 3 5 7 9 10 8 6 4 2

Other Titles by Andrew G. Nelson

<u>James Maguire Series</u>

Perfect Pawn

Queen's Gambit

Bishop's Gate

Knight Fall

<u>Alex Taylor Series</u>

Small Town Secrets

Little Boy Lost

<u>NYPD Cold Case Series</u>

The Katherine White Murder

<u>Non- Fiction</u>

Uncommon Valor – Insignia of the NYPD ESU

Uncommon Valor II– Challenge Coins of the NYPD ESU

DEDICATION

To my wife Nancy, without your love, support and constant encouragement this book would not have been possible.

Thank you for always believing in me.

To Chuck, whose friendship and guidance fueled my appreciation for the *history* of the job. You are sorely missed every single day, my friend. Fidelis Ad Mortem.

To the men and women of the NYPD's Emergency Service Unit. You are truly the epitome of: *NY's Finest.*

And to God, through whom all things are possible.

Romans 8:28

ACKNOWLEDGEMENTS

It is not enough to present a collection of items for the reader to ogle over. While pleasing to the eye, it is the people and the stories behind the insignia that are the crucial component. This book seeks to merge the two, offering the reader an insight into the insignia as well as those who have designed them with honor.

This book would not have been possible without the assistance of a great many individuals, including numerous members of ESU, both active and retired. They provided me with not only a treasure trove of information, but something equally as precious: their time.

I would like to take this moment to extend my sincere thanks to the following:

Names Appear in Alphabetical Order

Tony Agugliaro, Patrick Barry, Andy Bershad, Dave Brink, Brian Brown, Dennis Cannale, Benny Colecchia, Mike Dazi, Frank Ferrara, John Flynn, Rich Gundacker, Dave Halinski, John Ippolito, Rob Isernia, Chuck King, Bill Kingston, Peter Knudsen, Chuck Kobel, George Krant, Donald LaSala, Tom Lia, Tony Lisi, Tom Longa, Jerry Maier, Vinny Manco, Rick Martinez, James McEniry, John McKenna, Tony Michalek, Sean Mulcahy, David Norman, Ryan Norman, Mike O'Neill, Frank Pinto, Mike Riso, Tony Sanpietro, Roger Savage, Evan Schwerner, Shawn Soler, Charles Steiger, Mike Taggert, Tatyana Timoshenko, Kathy Vigiano, Pete Whalen & Matt Zucker

IN MEMORIUM

The first recorded ESU officer who died in the line of duty was Patrolman William Kertin, ESU Squad 1. He was killed on July 28th, 1929, from injuries he sustained in an auto accident. The ESU truck that he was riding in had been responding to an alarm, when it struck a bus. Kertin was killed and four other ESU officers were injured.

At the time of this printing there have been a total of thirty-eight (38) ESU officers who have died as a result of injuries sustained in the line of duty. This number includes the fourteen (14) who were killed in the terrorist attack at the World Trade Center on September 11th, 2001.

It should be noted that the last eight officers listed below died as a result of illnesses directly attributed to the September 11th, attack. Sadly, it is a cruel reality that the lingering health issues from that event will continue to claim victims, well into the future.

I think that it is fitting that this book honors every ESU officer who has paid the ultimate price. Their sacrifice is the embodiment of the NYPD Motto: *Fidelis Ad Mortem* (Latin for: Faithful Unto Death).

- Ptl. William A. Kertin – July 28th, 1929
- Sgt. George Nadler – February 1st, 1935
- Ptl. Joseph J. McBreen – August 11th, 1937
- Ptl. Alexander C. Stutt – June 9th, 1939
- Ptl. Francis M. O'Hara – November 25th, 1946
- Ptl. Peter J. Knudsen – November 25th, 1946
- Lt. Charles R. Michie – November 25th, 1946

- Ptl. Charles A. Brereton – September 30th, 1947
- Ptl. Kenneth L. Cozier – April 19th, 1963
- Ptl. John Banks – April 15th, 1968
- Ptl. Salvatore Spinola – October 2nd, 1969
- Ptl. Patrick O'Connor – November 24th, 1971
- P.O. Stephen Gilroy – January 19th, 1973
- P.O. Joseph McCormack – September 29th, 1983
- P.O. Francis LaSala – January 10th, 1987
- Sgt. John Coughlin – September 11th, 2001
- Sgt. Rodney Gillis – September 11th, 2001
- Sgt. Michael Curtin – September 11th, 2001
- P.O. Jerome Dominguez – September 11th, 2001
- P.O. Walter Weaver – September 11th, 2001
- P.O. Ronald Kloepfer – September 11th, 2001
- P.O. Thomas Langone – September 11th, 2001
- P.O. Vincent Danz – September 11th, 2001
- P.O. Joseph Vigiano – September 11th, 2001
- P.O. Stephen Driscoll – September 11th, 2001
- P.O. Santos Valentin – September 11th, 2001
- P.O. Paul Talty – September 11th, 2001
- P.O. John D'Allara– September 11th, 2001
- P.O. Brian McDonnell – September 11th, 2001
- Sgt. Keith Ferguson – January 31st, 2004
- Capt. Barry Galfano – June 26th, 2011 *
- Lt. Christopher Pupo – June 23rd, 2012 *
- Capt. Dennis Morales – July 27th, 2012 *
- P.O. Anthony Mangiaracina – September 10th, 2012 *
- Sgt. Patrick P. Murphy – August 20th, 2014 *
- Det. Louis Fernandez – October 16th, 2014 *
- Deputy Chief James Molloy – January 30th, 2017 *
- Det. Christian Lindsay – February 12th, 2017*

* Was a Member of ESU at the time of the 9/11 attack and developed illness as a result of that assignment.

TABLE OF CONTENTS

FOREWORD

"When the public needs help they call the police, when the police need help they call ESU."

While I was in the process of finishing work on my book: *Uncommon Valor – Insignia of the NYPD Emergency Service Unit*, an explosion occurred within the NYPD collecting community in the form of challenge coins. At the time I was faced with a dilemma. Should I put the insignia book on hold, while I tried to navigate this new field of interest, or proceed with publishing it? I chose the former, as I knew that this new field would require much more research to properly investigate.

For decades, cloth insignia had been the preferred method of establishing unit *esprit-de-corps*. This first began to change back in the late 90's when the first ESU challenge coins were minted. Even so, it would take more then a decade for coins to finally begin making in-roads in the previously patch dominated collecting world.

After the attack of September 11th, other units began to produce coins, not just in ESU, but throughout the NYPD as a whole. In an amazing turn of events, over the last few years the number of coins being produced by individual commands far exceeds the number of patches produced over the last few *decades*.

The proliferation of challenge coins has been greatly attributed to a growing roll call of former military personnel within the NYPD. It is from within the various military branches that the popularity of challenge coins has its base.

After much research, I decided that the extensive amount of coins that have been, and continue to be, created deserved their own separate book which I am honored to present to you now.

Sgt. Andrew G. Nelson, NYPD (Ret.)
Edinburg, Illinois – February 2017

HISTORY OF THE CHALLENGE COIN

While it is nearly impossible to determine when and where the tradition of challenge coins began, one story dates back to World War 1. During the war, American volunteers from all parts of the country filled the newly formed flying squadrons in Europe. Many of these young officers were from well-to-do families. In one squadron, a wealthy lieutenant ordered medallions struck in solid bronze and presented them to his unit. As the story goes, one young pilot placed the medallion in a small leather pouch that he wore about his neck. Shortly after acquiring the medallion, the pilot's aircraft was severely damaged by ground fire. He was forced to land behind enemy lines and was immediately captured by a German patrol. In order to discourage his escape, the Germans took all of his personal identification except for the small leather pouch around his neck. In the meantime, he was taken to a small French town near the front. Taking advantage of a bombardment that night, he escaped. However, he was without any personal identification.

He succeeded in avoiding German patrols by donning civilian attire and reached the front lines. With great difficulty, he crossed *no-man's land.* Eventually, he stumbled onto a French outpost. Unfortunately, saboteurs had plagued the French in the sector. They sometimes masqueraded as civilians and wore civilian clothes. Not recognizing the young pilot's American accent, the French thought him to be a saboteur and made ready to execute him. He had no identification to prove his allegiance, but he did have his leather pouch containing the medallion. He showed the medallion to his would-be executioners and, as luck would have it, one of his French captors recognized the squadron insignia on the medallion. They delayed his execution long enough for him to confirm his identity and instead of shooting him they gave him a bottle of wine.

It became tradition to ensure that all members carried their medallion at all times. This was accomplished through a *challenge* in the following manner: a challenger would ask to see the medallion. If the challenged person could not produce their medallion, they were required to buy a drink of choice for the member who had challenged them. If, however, the challenged member did produce his medallion, then the challenging member was required to pay for the drink.

During the Korean War, Col. William 'Buffalo Bill' Quinn, of the 17th Infantry Regiment, had actual coins made for his men. It featured a buffalo on one side, a nod to its creator, and the Regiment's insignia on the other. A hole was drilled in the top so the men could wear it around their necks, instead of in a leather pouch.

In Vietnam, things took a decidedly *darker* turn in the form of *bullet clubs*, whose members carried a single, personalized, unused bullet at all times. Many of these bullets were given as a reward for surviving a mission, with the idea that it was now a 'last resort bullet,' to be used on yourself, instead of surrendering if defeat seemed imminent.

Of course carrying a bullet quickly became a show of *machismo*, so what had originally started off as handgun or M16 rifle round, soon escalated to .50 caliber bullets, anti-aircraft rounds, and even artillery shells, in an effort to one-up each other. Unfortunately, when a challenge was presented, it meant they were slamming live ammunition down on the table.

Concerned that a deadly 'accident' might occur, commands soon banned ordnance from being used, choosing to replace it with a *Special Forces* coin instead. Soon nearly every unit had their own coin, and some even minted commemorative coins for hard-fought battles to hand out to those who lived to tell the tale. The loss of a coin was, and remains, tantamount to eternal disgrace and banishment.

CHALLENGE COIN RULES

While there are many variations to this theme, the following list outlines the generally accepted rules governing both the challenge coin and as well as acceptable challenges.

1. Rules of the challenge coin game must be given or explained to all new coin holders.

2. The coin MUST be carried at all times. You can be challenged for it anywhere, at any time, and you must produce the coin without taking more than four steps (considered to be within arm's reach) to produce it.

3. When challenging, the challenger must state whether it is for a single drink or a round of drinks.

4. Failure to produce a coin, for whatever reason, results in the challenged person purchasing the round or single (whatever the challenger stated). Once the offender (coinless challenge) has bought the drink or round, they can't be challenged again.

5. If all that are challenged produce their coins, the challenger loses and must buy the drinks for all respondents.

6. Under no circumstances can a coin be handed to another person who has been challenged.

7. If a coin is lost, replacement is up to the individual. A new coin should be acquired at the earliest opportunity. Loss of a coin, and not replacing it, doesn't relieve a member of his or her responsibilities under challenge.

8. There are no exceptions to the rules. They apply at all times, whether the challenged person is clothed or un-clothed. At the time of a challenge you are permitted one step and an arm's reach to locate your coin.

9. It must be a coin. Coins forged into unit belt buckles, key chains or necklaces do not count. No holes may be drilled into a coin. An otherwise unmarred coin, worn in a holder around the neck, is valid.

10. The coin should be controlled at all times.

THE BIRTH OF ESU

No book about the insignia of ESU would be complete without first establishing the history of this vaunted unit.

In 1964, the Philadelphia Police Department established what became known as the *first* official Special Weapons and Tactics (SWAT) team in the United States. Three years later, the Los Angeles Police Department launched their SWAT team. These were the first units dedicated to specifically addressing escalating violence in urban areas. Without taking anything away from these two premier agencies, in my opinion, they were about four decades late to the party.

In April 1930, the New York City Police Department's, Emergency Service Division (ESD), was *officially* created. While the Division was started on that date, the foundation of the Police Emergency Service can actually be traced back several years earlier to 1925.

In fact, if one were to look at the history in totality, you would follow a lineage that goes back to the days of the old Police Reserve Squads; which were formed after the American Civil War to deal with riots. These reserves consisted of officers who were assigned *extra duty* to supplement the regular patrol force, in the event of a public disturbance.

After WWI, a growing climate of social unrest led to rioting in more than three dozen U.S. cities in the summer of 1919. It revealed the need for a specialized, highly trained unit to respond to these events. This led to the creation of the NYPD's Riot Battalion. The personnel of the Riot Battalion, also sometimes referred to as the *Riot Regiment*, was composed of members of the Police Department who had actual military experience, and who were thoroughly versed in the handling and use of firearms, as well as various other implements of warfare.

As originally conceived, the Riot Battalion consisted of four companies: 'A', 'B', 'C', and 'D'. Each company was headed by a Captain, 3 Lieutenants, 7 Sergeants and 104 Patrolmen. During the era of Prohibition, a 'Machine Gun' Company was added, and was staffed with a Captain, 4 Sergeants and 72 Patrolmen. Its primary role was addressing the rise in organized crime activity, including illegal breweries.

As time progressed, the need for a unit focused primarily on riots and crowd control began to diminish. A steadily growing population, coupled with increases in urban construction and a diversifying system of transportation, began to present new issues that the regular patrol officers simply could not begin to handle effectively. It soon became obvious that there was a need to have a specialized unit, which would be available to respond to the new type of emergency situations that New York City was beginning to face.

Police officers were now being forced to contend with a myriad of issues, such as gas leaks, pedestrians being run over by vehicles or falling from elevated train lines, and horses that would fall into open construction sites. As a result, protocols were developed that directed the reserve officers of the Riot Battalions to respond to these types of emergency calls, when they were not assigned to riot or crowd control duties.

This program proved to be so effective, that on July 7th, 1925, New York City Police Commissioner Richard E. Enright issued a formal order establishing two dedicated 'Emergency Automobile Squads'. Enright authorized the purchase of two, custom built, 1925 White Motor Company trucks.

These vehicles were equipped with all the necessary equipment to handle any emergency which might occur. The original trucks were enamel blue in color and had the lettering 'EMERGENCY SERVICE' written in gold lettering on the side.

White Motor Co. Truck circa late 1920's.

The Emergency Automobile Squad combined the duties of a rescue unit, *Pulmotor* (Oxygen) truck, riot platoon, first-aid, and motorized patrol. Each squad was designated to respond to all fires of two alarms or more, riots, train wrecks, serious automobile collisions, and any other emergencies where there were serious injuries or people were likely to die.

Initially, the coverage of the city was divided up amongst the two squads, which were comprised of six sergeants and forty-four officers.

While the original recommendation was for a lieutenant to be in charge of each squad, there are no personnel records of any lieutenants actually being transferred into Emergency Service until the division was formed in 1930.

- Emergency Automobile Squad #1 was quartered at 138 West 30th Street in Manhattan and was assigned to respond to emergencies in the boroughs of Manhattan and the Bronx. The officers reported to, and were under the supervision of, the Commanding Officer of the 7th Precinct.

- Emergency Automobile Squad #2 was quartered in Brooklyn at 298 Classon Avenue and was assigned to respond to emergencies in the boroughs of Brooklyn and Queens. The officers reported to, and were under the supervision of, the Commanding Officer of the 46th Precinct.

The following list contains the names of the original fifty members of the Emergency Automobile Squad, as established by NYPD Special Order #171 dated 07/06/1925:

Emergency Automobile #1

Sergeant:

Sgt. James M. Gordon Jr.
Sgt. Joseph A. Stanton
Sgt. John F. Ward

Patrolmen:

William J. Bak
Otto W. Behrens
John J. Boyle
Frank A. Dineen
Daniel J. Flynn
Henry Fleuchaus
John J. Hartnett
James A. Irving Jr.
Frederick Kahrig
William Kaval
Daniel F. Kerrigan
Francis M. Kelly
Albert E. Latchford
George C. Moench
John D. Paar
Frederick L. Pfeiffer
Edward F. Powers
Frederick H. Sorger
Laurence H. Spitzen
Joseph Theuer
John Tormey

Emergency Automobile #2

Sergeant:

Sgt. Ulysses E. Beotig
Sgt. David Geraghty
Sgt. Joseph Green

Patrolmen:

Ernest M. Emann
Charles Frailer
John J. Hartnett
James F. O'Brien
Francis J. Donnelly
Charles Dosch
Joseph V. DeSoucey
William Ferri
Michael P. Higgins
Edward O. Junginger
Charles P. Klein
Charles E. Kraemer
Walter G. Lagarenne
Edward B. Lahey
Edwin L. Lundin
Joseph F. Motjenbacker
Ernest Peters
Edward F. Powers
Thomas C. Regan
John M. Simerlein
Arthur F. Walz
Albert L. Williamson
Edward Unger

On September 16th, 1926, based upon the success of the inaugural two Emergency Automobile Squads, Police Commissioner George McLaughlin ordered that a third squad, comprised of three sergeants and nineteen officers, be organized and put into service. The name of the unit was also officially changed from the Emergency Automobile Squad to the Emergency Service Squad.

- Emergency Service Squad #3 was quartered in the Bronx at 820 Washington Avenue and was assigned to respond to emergencies in the Bronx. The officers reported to the Commanding Officer of the 19th Pct.

On November 3rd, 1926, the officers of Emergency Service engaged in their first major gun battle when NYC mobster, Herman 'Hyman' Amberg, who was in jail for the murder of a local jeweler, attempted to escape from the old 'Tombs' jail on Centre Street, along with two other prisoners. Pistols had been previously smuggled into the jail for the three men. They faked illnesses so that they would be brought to the jail doctor. Once inside the doctor's office, they pulled their guns and attempted to escape. Newly assigned Warden, Peter Mallon, heard the commotion and came running to stop the escape. He was shot and killed as he entered the office.

The three inmates then fled into the prison courtyard, near the Lafayette Street gate, where they exchanged shots with Keeper (the former title for Corrections Officer) Jeremiah Murphy and his partner, Daniel O'Connor. Keeper Murphy was killed and his partner was wounded.

Emergency Service responded and engaged the inmates from nearby buildings, raking the jail from all sides with heavy machine gun fire and gas bombs.

The gun battle at the Tombs went on for thirty minutes, with hundreds of rounds being fired. Amberg and the other two inmates hunkered down behind a pile of coal in the yard, before making their way to the safety of a guardhouse. They occasionally returned fire, wounding a police officer and a businessman in the Conklin Building across the street. At some point, two of the inmates were shot and wounded. With no escape possible, all three committed suicide.

On May 4th, 1928, Police Commissioner Joseph A. Warren, issued General Order #11 which doubled the number of squads in service, creating new Squads 4, 5 & 6. Each squad was manned by three sergeants and twenty-one officers.

This expansion resulted in a redistricting of the service areas for these units, as well as a relocation of quarters for Squad #2. These squads, and their vehicles, were assigned to the following precincts:

- Emergency Squad #1 was quartered in the 7th Precinct at 138 West 30th Street in Manhattan. It was assigned to respond to emergencies in Manhattan, south of 86th Street, including all of Central Park and the Borough of Richmond.
- Emergency Squad #2 was relocated to the 15th Precinct, at 1854 Amsterdam Avenue in Manhattan. It was assigned to respond to emergencies in Manhattan, north of 86th Street, excluding of Central Park.
- Emergency Squad #3 was quartered in the 19th Precinct at 3rd Avenue and 160th Street in the Bronx. It was assigned to respond to all emergencies in the Bronx.
- Emergency Squad #4 (Formerly Squad 2) was quartered in the 42-A Precinct, located at 653 Grand Avenue in Brooklyn. It was assigned to respond to all emergencies in Brooklyn, except within the boundaries of the 44th, 48-A, 49th, 49-A, 50th, 51st, and 51-A Precincts.
- Emergency Squad #5 was quartered in the 59th Precinct Station House, located at 85 Fourth Street, Long Island City, Queens. It was assigned to respond to all emergencies in the 59th and 64th Precincts in Queens as

well as the 48-A, 49th, 49-A, 50th, 51st, and 51-A Precincts in Brooklyn.

- Emergency Squad #6 was quartered in the 56th Precinct at 275 Church Street in Richmond Hill, Queens. It was assigned to respond to all emergencies in Queens, except the 59th and 64th Precincts, as well as the 44th Precinct in Brooklyn.

POLICE DEPARTMENT

CITY OF NEW YORK

OFFICE OF THE POLICE COMMISSIONER

New York, May 4, 1928.

GENERAL ORDERS NO. 11.

POLICE EMERGENCY SERVICE

General Orders No. 26, 1926, is hereby amended to read:

1. Police Emergency Service is hereby established, and shall consist of automobiles with emergency equipment and trained crews. This service is established for the purpose of getting members of the Force of this Department to the scene of an emergency in the shortest time possible to establish police lines and perform such other duty as may be required at large fires, riots, strikes or catastrophies. The Police Emergency Service Squads, when on duty, must at all times be prepared to respond instantly.

2. Upon arriving at the scene of an emergency the commanding officer of the Police Emergency Service Squad will immediately establish police lines, take charge of and be responsible for the distribution of all members of the Force who respond to the emergency until the arrival of an officer of higher rank. He will immediately inform the commanding officer of the Telegraph Bureau of the nature of the occurrence and the number of additional reserves required, if any.

3. The commanding officer at the scene of an emergency will release the Police Emergency Squad as soon as their services can be dispensed with, promptly notifying the Telegraph Bureau of such action. The commanding officer of the Police Emergency Squad will immediately notify the Telegraph Bureau of their return to quarters.

4. The Police Emergency Service will be installed in the following precincts and will be an integral part of such commands, and will cover the territory specified:

Police Emergency Service No. 1.

7th Precinct, 138 West 30th Street, Manhattan

All that territory within the Borough of Manhattan, south of 86th Street, including Central Park, and the Borough of Richmond.

Police Emergency Service No. 2

15th Precinct, 1854 Amsterdam Avenue, Manhattan

All that territory within the Borough of Manhattan, north of 86th Street, except Central Park.

Police Emergency Service No. 3

19th Precinct, 3d Avenue and 160th Street, The Bronx

All that territory within the Borough of The Bronx.

Police Emergency Service No. 4

42-A Precinct, 653 Grand Avenue, Borough of Brooklyn

All that territory within the Borough of Brooklyn, except within the boundaries of the 44th, 48-A, 49th, 49-A, 50th, 51st and 51-A Precincts.

Police Emergency Service No. 5

59th Precinct, 85 Fourth Street, Long Island City, Queens

All that territory within the 59th and 64th Precincts, Borough of Queens, and that within the boundaries of the 48-A, 49th, 49-A 50th, 51st and 51-A Precincts, Borough of Brooklyn.

Police Emergency Service No. 6

56th Precinct, 275 Church Street, Richmond Hill, Queens

All that territory within the 44th Precinct, Borough of Brooklyn, and all of the Borough of Queens, except that within the boundaries of the 59th and 64th Precincts.

5. A sergeant designated by the Police Commissioner shall be in command of each Police Emergency Service Squad.

6. The force assigned to each such Police Emergency Service will be known as the Police Emergency Service Squad and will work according to the regular Patrolmen's Duty Chart. Sergeants in command of Police Emergency Service No. 1 and No. 4 will be assigned to the 1st, 4th and 7th Squads, and Sergeants in command of Police Emergency Service No. 2 and No. 5 will be assigned to the 2d, 5th and 8th Squads, and Sergeants in command of Police Emergency Service No. 3 and No. 6 will be assigned to the 3d, 6th and 9th squads. At least two patrolmen of the Police Emergency Service Squad will be assigned to each squad of the Patrolmen's Duty Chart. Vacancies will be filled as provided by the Rules and Regulations. Assignments to the Police Emergency Service will not be changed for any reason, except with the approval of the Police Commissioner.

7. Commanding Officers of precincts to which this emergency service is assigned will provide necessary accomodations for the automobile and squads.

8. A blotter will be kept in which will be entered all calls and all active police duty performed by the Police Emergency Service Squads. This does not include roll calls, etc., which will be kept in the Precinct Blotter.

9. These Police Emergency Service Automobiles with crews will proceed to the scene of any Police Emergency as directed by the Chief Inspector, or Deputy Chief Inspector at Police Headquarters. They will also proceed to the scene of fires on second alarms received from fire signal stations. They will answer first alarms only when so directed.

10. The Fire Department call for Police Emergency Service will be a preliminary ten strokes, followed by ten strokes, followed by the fire station number where desired, followed by the number of the Police Emergency Service wanted.

Effective 8 A. M., May 5, 1928.

JOSEPH A. WARREN,
Police Commissioner.

By 1929, the Department had reached the conclusion that, in order to better utilize them, the individual units should be removed from the control of the precinct commanders and transferred under the direct command of a qualified superior officer.

EMERGENCY SERVICE

The Emergency Service of this Department consists of 11 trucks, specially equipped with the following equipment:

The personnel consists of 33 Sergeants, and 231 Patrolmen.

During the past year this service was reorganized and enlarged by the addition of 8 trucks; 24 Sergeants and 168 Patrolmen.

9 additional trucks will be added to this unit during January, 1930, necessitating the assignment of 27 Sergeants and 189 Patrolmen.

In this reorganization, the widely scattered trucks, operating as separate units, will be formed into one distinct division, and the responsibility of control and supervision will be taken from the commanding officers of the precincts in which the trucks are housed and placed on a superior officer who will be assigned to assume charge.

It was found that the commanding officers of precincts lacked training and experience in the care and use of equipment and the work of the crews and were incapable of properly inspecting the trucks and equipment or in other ways exercising supervision.

The necessity of a superior at the head of this unit was further emphasized by confusion and resultant delay in the acquisition of supplies or new equipment. It was left to the individual members of the squads to keep themselves informed on innovations in rescue methods, first aid to the injured and other details of their work.

Annual Report – Police Department City of New York (1929)

On April 10th, 1930, Police Commissioner Grover A. Whalen issued General Order #20, which created the Emergency Service Division and Inspector Daniel A. Kerr was assigned as the first commanding officer. Inspector Kerr, also known as ‘Iron Dan’, held the distinction of being the strongest man in the NYPD. Kerr won the title after emerging victorious from a wrestling match against fellow officer, and former professional weightlifter, Selig “Ajax” Whitman.

At the time, Kerr wanted to get away from what he perceived to be the more *violent* chapters of the unit’s history in dealing with riots. He envisioned a more service oriented unit and created the axiom ‘*At*

Your Service'. Over the years, this saying faded away, replaced with the more appropriate: '*Anytime, Anywhere, Anyplace*'.

By this time the number of Emergency Service Squads had been increased from six to twenty. In June of 1930, ESD commenced its own emergency service school at the police academy. This two week intense course was designed to prepare incoming members for the rigors of Emergency Service work.

By the mid 1930's the division had also absorbed the Aviation Bureau and Harbor Unit, giving it a unique *land*, *sea* and *air* capability. By the early 1950's the division would reduce the number of squads by half, resulting in the current 10 Squad structure that remains in place today.

Over time, the nomenclature would change from Emergency Service Division (ESD) to Emergency Service Section (ESS) and finally to Emergency Service Unit (ESU).

In June 1973, both the Aviation and Harbor units became autonomous entities. That same year saw the first female officer, Ann Morrissey, a nursing specialist, assigned to ESU.

The next major change in ESU occurred in 1995, when the NYC Housing and Transit Police Departments were merged into the NYPD. With this merger, the personnel of the HAPD and TAPD Emergency Rescue Units were absorbed into ESU.

One of the aspects which set ESU apart from other tactical units around the country is the fact that the officers of ESU are tasked with responding to every conceivable emergency situation. They are called upon to handle everything from plane crashes and building collapses, to persons threatening to jump from bridges. There simply are no *typical* days for ESU officers. They have literally seen and done everything.

When an officer on patrol encounters something he can't handle, the call goes out to send ESU. On any given day ESU officers can go from a *pin job*, a motor vehicle accident with a person trapped inside, to an armed barricaded emotionally disturbed person. The vehicles they travel in contain equipment that make them look like a mobile version of *Home Depot* and *Guns-R-Us*.

The training program for ESU officers includes the following:

- Bridge & Building Rescues
- Vehicle & Train Accident Extrication
- Building Collapse Extrication
- Rigging & Line Techniques
- Welding / Torch Techniques
- First Aid / Emergency Medical Technician
- Non-Lethal Weapons
- Power Tool Operation
- Elevator / Escalator Rescue
- Animal Control
- Water Rescue
- Helicopter Rescue / Rappel / Medevac
- Bomb / IED Recognition
- HAZMAT / Chemical Agents
- Dignitary Protection Operations
- Specialized Vehicle Operations
- Hostage Rescue
- Emotionally Disturbed Persons
- SCUBA
- Electrical / Gas Emergencies
- Aircraft Emergency / Rescue
- Forcible / Barricaded Entry Techniques
- High Rise Structure Rescues
- Department of Correction Emergencies
- Self-Contained Breathing Apparatus

- Auxiliary Generators / Lighting
- Specialized Weapons Training

All of this, while still maintaining a routine patrol function.

Today, the Emergency Service Unit is divided into ten *trucks*, the name colloquially used to describe the ten individual commands that are tasked with providing coverage throughout the five boroughs of New York City.

- Truck 1 (Manhattan)
- Truck 2 (Manhattan)
- Truck 3 (Bronx)
- Truck 4 (Bronx)
- Truck 5 (Staten Island)
- Truck 6 (Brooklyn)
- Truck 7 (Brooklyn)
- Truck 8 (Brooklyn)
- Truck 9 (Queens)
- Truck 10 (Queens)

Each of these commands use two distinct types of vehicles. The large 'Truck,' which usually remains at the quarters unless summoned for a big job, and three smaller Radio Emergency Patrol vehicles, or *REP*'s. These smaller trucks are used for routine patrol and initial emergency response. Their radio call signs are 'Adam', 'Boy', and 'Charlie'.

Photo courtesy of Tom O'Connor

ESU COINS

The first ESU coins appeared back in the late 1990's. At that time, challenge coins were somewhat of a novelty within the NYPD, so the introduction of these coins was quite unique, especially for collectors. However, by their very nature, it is not unusual that ESU would have been at the vanguard of this new wave. They had been pioneers, in one form or another, throughout their storied history.

Many of the members of ESU had served in the military, where the tradition of challenge coins first began, so it was only fitting that they would look to incorporate this type of fraternal insignia into this close knit, highly specialized unit.

After the September 11th terror attack, memorial coins began to appear, recognizing the ESU members that had been lost on that day. However, it would be another dozen or so years until the real surge in coins would begin.

Just as ESU played a pivotal role, years before, in developing individual unit patches, they would also be at the forefront of introducing challenge coins.

The first coins to emerge were primarily created within the ten individual 'Trucks' spread out throughout New York City. Eventually the practice would extend to the specialized units such as the A-Team and Counter Sniper. As of today, every unit is represented by a coin.

This book details all of the *authorized* coins that have been used by ESU. Also included are certain memorial coins, from non-ESU commands, which honor members of ESU who have died.

Two notes before we begin:

First, there are numerous ways to describe the base metal component of each coin. For the purpose of this book, and to avoid confusion, any polished or chrome finish is simply described by its color, i.e.: silver, gold. Any matte style finish is referred to as *antique* silver or *antique* gold.

The second is offered up as a warning to collectors. One of the most difficult aspects of this book was photographing the respective coins. What started off as a simple task soon became the bane of my literary existence. I found myself photographing coins with my Canon camera, as well as my cell phone. Indoor, outdoor, natural light, diffused light, hell I even tried a desk lamp and my kitchen lights; all in order to chase that elusive photo and capture the truest image of the item in front of the lens hand. At this point I am firmly convinced there is a special place in hell for the creator of chrome.

My adventure in metallic photography taught me a very good lesson, one that I had not encountered in the photography for my ESU insignia book. The coin details you see in a photo are not always representative of the piece. As evidence, I submit the following:

The Truck 6 coin on the left was shot using my Galaxy S7 cellphone, on my desk, with natural light. The coin on the right was shot outside, using my Canon SX30 digital camera and diffused natural light. Despite the many differences between the two coins, they are in fact the same coin.

As a collector myself, I cannot stress enough the importance of always knowing your subject and not relying solely on the photos you are provided.

TRUCK ONE (MANHATTAN)

In 2005, Detective John McKenna tasked *Huntzman Enterprises* to come up with the artwork for the first Truck 1 challenge coin.

The 1.75" round, silver coin featured the unit's patch design on the obverse with the lettering: Truck One / Manhattan along the border. In the center is the NYC skyline, with the Twin Towers, and the unit's stylized '1' & lightning bolt logo.

Proposed artwork for 1st issue coin

The three gold stars on the obverse side memorialize the police officers from Truck 1 that had been killed in the line of duty: Frank LaSala, Patrick O'Connor, and Brian McDonnell.

Patrolman Patrick O'Connor died in the line of duty on November 24th, 1971. O'Connor and his partner had been returning from Truck 6 when they stopped to aide a motorist on the Gowanus Expressway. While sitting in their REP it was struck by an oil truck.

Officer Frank LaSala died in the line of duty on January 10th, 1987, in a building fire several buildings away from Truck 1's quarters. When alerted to the fire, Officer LaSala donned a *SCOT* air pack and proceeded to the location where he rescued a number of residents before he became trapped.

Officer Brian McDonnell died in the line of duty on September 11th, 2001, in the terror attack on the World Trade Center.

On the reverse is a regulation ESU patch, superimposed over two American flags, with an eagle perched on top of it, along with the lettering: Emergency Service Unit / Est. 1930, on the outer ring.

1st Issue coin

Later that same year, Detective Sean Mulcahy had *Huntzman Enterprises* produce a *members only* challenge coin. This new coin was the same as the previous design, but was produced in gold metal.

1st Issue - Members only coin

In 2010, a prototype set of coins, done in antique gold and silver, were produced for Detective Mulcahy, by *Huntzman Enterprises*. The prototypes were intended to be a 2nd issue, with the silver being for general use and the gold for *members only*, however this design was rejected in favor of the previous polished version.

Prototype - Antique silver coin

Prototype - Antique gold members coin

In 2011, Detective Mulcahy had *Warrior Chips* produce a 1.75" poker chip for Truck 1. The obverse featured the Truck 1 patch logo and the reverse featured an ESU patch, superimposed over an American Flag, with the lettering: Emergency Service Unit – Anytime Baby!!

1st Issue 'Poker Chip'

In 2014, two new coins were produced for Truck 1. Both were the same 1.75" size and bore the same basic design elements as the original coin. The major difference between these and the original is the use of hard enamel on these new coins.

The first coin produced was done in antique silver; similar to the prototype done back in 2010. On this version of the coin the outer enamel ring on the obverse side was changed to a navy blue color and the black enamel detailing in the lightning bolt and the letters: NYPD / 1 / ESU was removed. The reverse side of the coin did not have any enamel in the outer ring.

2nd Issue coin

Unfortunately, this modified design was not popular with the members of the unit and a second coin was produced. This antique silver coin was the same size, and featured the same design elements of the former coin, however, on this version the outer rings, on both sides, were done in black enamel like the original. Additionally, in this version the black enamel detailing in the lightning bolt and the letters: NYPD / 1 / ESU was added back in.

3rd Issue coin

In 2015, Detective Ryan Norman produced a new coin for the unit. This one was produced by *Gray Water Ops* and was a complete departure from the previous versions.

The 2" high, gold metal design is in the shape of the unit's large '1' & lightning bolt with three gold memorial stars. The obverse features the lettering: NYPD / ESU / Truck One / Manhattan on a white background with blue border.

On the reverse is the NYPD's Medal of Honor, on a black background, and the names of the three Truck 1 members who it had been awarded to: Ptlm. Patrick J. O'Connor, P.O. Francis J. LaSala, and P.O. Brian G. McDonnell with the NYPD Motto: *Fidelis Ad Mortem*. It also features a clear epoxy cover on both sides.

4th Issue coin

Due to high demand for the coin, a 2nd issue of this coin was produced in 2015 by Detective Norman. However, in the new run, the epoxy cover was left off.

4th Issue coin (without epoxy cover)

At the same time that the 2nd issue debuted, a *members only* version was also produced. This coin featured the same design elements, but this version had a green background on the obverse with a white border. In addition, this coin had a *security element* added to it in order to prevent it from being duplicated.

4th Issue - Members only coin (Photo courtesy Ryan Norman)

On a historical note, the original ‘1’ and lightning bolt logo design came about back in the 1980’s when several members of the unit wanted to have a large ‘1’ made to affix to the front of the truck.

As the story goes, Officer Frank LaSala had it made by a friend of his, but when they got it back the metal ‘1’ had a lightning bolt affixed to it. As a result, the lightning bolt has been part of the unit’s logo ever since.

While this logo no longer adorns the front of the truck, the original is still around, affixed to the Command Center door at the quarters of Truck 1.

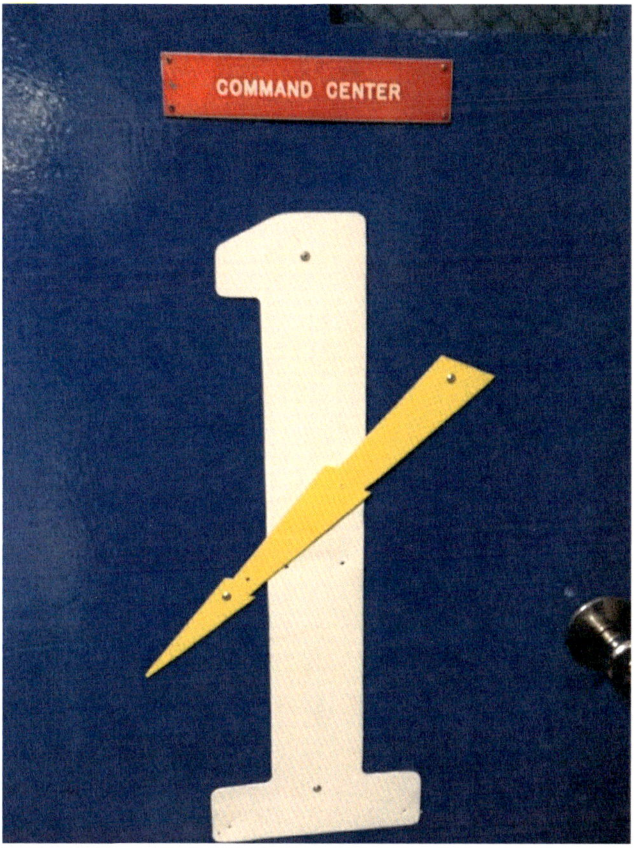

Photo courtesy of Andy Bershad

TRUCK TWO (MANHATTAN)

In 2002, Sergeant John Flynn collaborated with other members of Truck 2 to design and produce the unit's first challenge coin. The 1.75" round, silver metal design features a clear epoxy cover.

On the obverse side is the unit's patch design, a Tomcat in a tuxedo leaning on a 2, which had originally been produced by Detective Joe Vigiano in 1999. Along the border is the lettering: *Harlem*, the geographical area where Truck 2 is quartered, and, along the bottom edge, the names of the Truck 2 members who were killed in the line of duty: Sgt. Curtin, Det. Vigiano, PO D'Allara and PO McCormack.

The first three officers listed were killed in the September 11th terror attack and Officer McCormack was shot and killed in 1983 by an emotionally disturbed perpetrator. The four blue stars along the edge honor the fallen.

On the reverse side is the ESU patch, superimposed over an American flag with the lettering: Emergency Service Squad 2 / NYPD.

1st Issue coin

In 2015, Detective Michael Dazi had *Challenge Coins Ltd* produce a new Truck 2 challenge coin. The 2" round, silver metal coin featured many of the design elements of the previous design, but now there was a white background behind the Tomcat on the obverse side with the lettering: Harlem / Truck Two. In addition, the blue stars were also changed to white and there was no epoxy cover over the top.

On the reverse side, the ESU patch was now superimposed over an NYPD flag with the lettering: Emergency Service Squad 2 / Anytime Anywhere. The first run of these coins were factory numbered, but later versions where not.

2nd Issue coin

Also in 2015, Detective Michael Dazi had *Challenge Coins Ltd* produce a series of four *members only* Truck 2 challenge coins.

The 2" round, metal design featured the same elements of the general coin, but did not have any enamel coloring. Instead, these coins utilized a unique pattern of different color metal finishes to denote the differences. While they appear similar to the color version, they are in fact from a different mold and feature a *security element* to prevent it from being duplicated.

These new coins recognized the following categories: 1st year member, 5th year member, 10th year member and 15th year / retired member.

The 1st year member coin featured an antique copper toned base with gold tone lettering, stars, '2' and ESU truck.

1st Year - Members only coin

The 5th year member coin featured an antique gold toned base with silver tone lettering, stars, '2' and ESU truck.

5th Year - Members only coin

The 10th year member coin featured an antique silver toned base with gold tone lettering, stars, '2' and ESU truck.

10b Year - Members only coin

The 15th year / Retired member coin featured a gold toned base with copper tone lettering, stars, '2' and ESU truck.

15th Year / Retired - Members only coin

Later in 2015, Detective Dazi had *Challenge Coins Ltd* produce a new, subdued version of the Truck 2 challenge coin. All of the color enamel was removed from the silver metal design and replaced by black enamel

2nd Issue subdued coin

In 2016, Detective Dazi had *Challenge Coins Ltd* produce a new version of the Truck 2 challenge coin. The 2" round, silver metal coin features the units original patch design with MoJo, their beloved Boxer mascot, sitting atop the Manhattanville Viaduct on the obverse. The coin retained the same design elements on the reverse side as the 2nd Issue coin.

3rd Issue 'Mojo' coin

TRUCK THREE (BRONX)

In the late 1990's the first Truck 3 challenge coin was designed and produced by members of the command. The 1.5" round, antique gold metal design featured a large number '3' with three stars on the obverse and the lettering: Police Department City of New York Emergency Service Squad Three.

On the reverse side is an ESU patch with the lettering: Anything Anytime Anywhere, along with the date: April 10, 1930, the recognized founding date of the Emergency Service Division. The blank space on the observe side had been intended as a place where a number or inscription could be placed.

1st Issue coin

In addition to the above design, an antique silver *members only* coin was also produced. The design remained the same as the above, but the number '3' and stars on the obverse side had green enamel. Additionally, the patch on the reverse side was in full color enamel.

1st Issue - Members only coin (Photo courtesy Dave Brink)

Around 2005, Detective Richard Gundacker had *Challenge Coins R Us* produce a re-issue of the 1st coin. While it maintained all the design elements of the original, it was produced on a different mold from a photo of the original, which would account for minor differences.

Around 2008, Detective Gundacker had an updated version of the truck's challenge coin produced by *Signature Coins*. The 1.5" round, antique gold metal coin kept the same design elements as the original, but now featured green enamel in the '3' and yellow enamel in the stars on the obverse.

2nd Issue coin (Photo courtesy of Richard Gundacker)

In 2014, Detectives Roger Savage and Richard Gundacker collaborated on a new Truck 3 challenge coin that was produced by *Signature Coins*.

The completely re-designed 2" round, antique silver coin features various elements that are integral to ESU's mission in the center of the obverse: a Medical Star of Life with a pair of M-4 rifles, jump wings, WMD logo, K9 Paw and a SCUBA helmet superimposed over it, with the legend 'SQUAD 3' and 'BRONX'. Along the outer border is the lettering: Police Department City of New York Emergency Service Unit.

The reverse side features the round ESU patch superimposed on top of crossed US and NYPD flags, in colored enamel, with the lettering: Anything Anytime Anywhere, along with the date: April 10, 1930. Three gold stars are spaced out around the center design.

3rd Issue coin

In 2015, Detective Roger Savage had *Signature Coins* produce a new version of the Truck 3 challenge coin. The design is the same size and features the same elements of the previous design, but this time a blue enamel background was placed behind the design elements on the obverse side. In addition, a new mold was used for the obverse and the lettering: Police

Department City of New York / Emergency Service Unit, is raised with a black enamel background.

4th Issue coin

In addition, a *members only* version was also produced. This style features the same design as the above issued coin, but has a green enamel background on the obverse.

4th Issue - Members only coin (Photo courtesy Roger Savage)

TRUCK FOUR (BRONX)

In 2006, Detective Evan Schwerner had *Quality Challenge Coins* produce the first Truck 4 challenge coin. The 1.75" round, silver metal design features a large green '4' with the word: Truck, in white, superimposed over an American flag, on the obverse. Along the border are two small stars and the lettering: Emergency Service Squad Four / Bronx.

On the reverse side is an ESU patch, superimposed over an NYPD flag, with the lettering: Police Department – City of New York, on the top and the NYPD Motto: Fidelis Ad Mortem, on the bottom. This coin has a clear epoxy cover.

1st Issue coin

In 2014, Detective Schwerner had *Northwest Territorial Mint* produce an updated version of the coin. The 1.75" round, silver metal design featured all the key elements of the prior design, but now featured the shields of the two Truck 4 members killed in the line of duty on September 11th, 2001: Sergeant John Coughlin and Police Officer Stephen Driscoll, flanking the '4'.

In addition, the background of the ESU patch on the reverse was now chrome silver. There was no epoxy cover used for this version.

2nd Issue coin

TRUCK FIVE (STATEN ISLAND)

In 2014, Detective Dennis Cannale had *All About Coins* produce the first Truck 5 challenge coin. The obverse of the 1.75" round, antique silver metal design features a tomcat, armed with an M-4 rifle, leaning on a green map of Staten Island. It is surrounded by logos indicating some of the work performed by ESU: Star of Life, HazMat placard, PADI flag, Rappel Wings, and the Jaws of Life.

The reverse side of the coin features an ESU patch, flanked by the U.S. and NYPD flags with the lettering: NYPD Special Operations Division / Emergency Service Squad 5.

1st Issue coin

In 2016, Sergeant Anthony Lisi and Detectives Michael Langan and Joseph Fermaint had *Gray Water Ops* produce the second Truck 5 challenge coin.

The 2.25" high, antique silver metal coin features the ESU patch on the obverse with the addition of a red number five at the bottom.

On the reverse is an image of the unit's truck, with crossed M-4 rifles underneath it and four stars. The stars represent four officers who died: two who were part of H.E.S.S.I. (Highway Emergency Service Staten Island) and two who had worked in Truck 5 and died from 9/11 related illness.

On the top of the coin is the Verrazano-Narrows Bridge with a helicopter hovering above it. This coin has an epoxy cover.

2nd Issue coin

TRUCK SIX (BROOKLYN)

In 2001, Detectives Jerome Maier and Pete Whalen designed and produced the first Truck 6. While the coin was originally done by Truck 6, the design was kept generic so that other units in ESU could also use it.

The 1.5" round, antique silver design was produced by *We Make Coins*. On the obverse is the original ESU Tomcat logo with the lettering: Emergency Service / Anytime, Baby…!

On the reverse is the ESU patch design with a small rectangular area that could be used to serialize or inscribe the coin.

1st Issue coin

In 2010, Sergeant Frank Ferrara had *Huntzman Enterprises* produce a new Truck 6 challenge coin. Initially, a gold and silver version was proposed, to denote *members only* and general issue, however this was later scrapped and only the silver version was produced.

Proposed artwork

The 1.75" round, silver metal coin featured the unit's shield shaped patch logo, an ESU truck with the Coney Island Parachute Jump and the Verrazano-Narrows Bridge in the background, with the lettering: NYPD /Truck 6, on the obverse. Along the outer border is the lettering: Emergency Service Unit / Brooklyn South.

On the reverse side is the traditional round ESU patch design.

2nd Issue coin (Blue border version without engine cowling)

The general issue version featured a blue border around the shield on the obverse while a second, members only version, was also produced. The members only one features a grey border around the shield.

2nd Issue coin (Grey border members only version without engine cowling)

Unfortunately, from the initial design stage to the mold scan stage an error occurred. As a result, the first batch of coins came back from the manufacturer with the engine cowling missing on the ESU truck. A second run, shown below, was produced in 2011 and corrected this error.

3rd Issue coin (Blue border version with engine cowling)

3rd Issue coin (Grey border members only version with engine cowling)

In 2015, Sergeant Ferrara, along with Detectives Pete Whalen, Mike Kennan and Steve Attarian, had a new coin produced for the truck by *Signature Coins*.

The 2" round, gold metal coin featured all of the design elements of the previous coin, but now featured a rope cut border. A gold star was also added into the patch logo, which memorialized Detective Luis Fernandez who died as a result of illness attributed to the September 11th attack.

4th Issue coin (Blue border version)

Like the previous coin, there were two issues: one with a blue border, which was made available to those outside the unit, and a 2nd version with a grey border, which was for *members only.*

*4th **Issue coin** (Grey border members only version – Photo courtesy Frank Ferrara)*

In addition, a separate memorial coin was produced honoring Detective Fernandez. The 2" gold coin features the blue border Truck 6 patch design on the obverse side. The reverse has Det. Fernandez's shield in the center along with his name on top and the NYPD motto underneath. It was only issued to members of Truck 6.

Det. Luis Fernandez memorial members only coin (Photo courtesy Frank Ferrara)

TRUCK SEVEN (BROOKLYN)

Detective Frank Pinto designed and produced the first Truck 7 challenge coin around 2005. The 1.5" round, silver metal coin featured a modified version of the unit's Tomcat & '7' logo on the obverse with the lettering: Feeling Lucky....? / ESU Truck 7. This had been the patch design previously done by Det. Joe Vigiano and his friend, David Smith, back in 1997.

On the reverse, superimposed over the American flag, were the names of the three Truck 7 members who had been killed in the line of duty: Police Officer's Ronald Kloepfer and Santos Valentin Jr., who died in the terror attack of September 11th, 2001 and Sergeant Keith Ferguson, who died on January 31st, 2004, during a foot pursuit. Along the border is the lettering: NYC Police Department / Emergency Service Unit.

1st Issue coin (Photo courtesy of Frank Pinto)

In 2008, Detective Al Gut had *Huntzman Enterprises* produce artwork for a proposed 2nd issue coin. The design incorporated elements of the unit's current patch design, which had also been produced by *Huntzman Enterprises,* on the obverse. It features three stars, representing the Truck 3 officers killed, along with the '5' and '2' dice and the legend:

Emergency Service Squad 7. Along the outer border is the lettering: Brooklyn / Anytime Baby!

On the reverse, superimposed over an NYPD flag, is the ESU patch with the lettering: Emergency Service Unit / Anytime, Anywhere, along the border. Unfortunately, at the time, production was never implemented on the design.

Proposed artwork for 2nd issue coin

Later in 2008, Detective Gut had *All About Coins* produce a 1.75" silver metal coin based on the original *Huntzman Enterprises* artwork.

2nd Issue coin

TRUCK EIGHT (BROOKLYN)

In 2011, Detective Dave Halinski had *All About Coins* produce the first Truck 8 challenge coin. The 2" round, silver metal design featured the unit's patch design, with the old blue Mack truck and the Williamsburg Bridge in the background, on the obverse with the lettering: Emergency Service Squad / Eight. On the outer border is the lettering Brooklyn North.

On the bottom portion of the obverse side is a small rectangular area. The first run of one hundred coins was sequentially numbered and many of these went to members assigned to the command. Subsequent runs of the coins were not serialized.

The reverse side features an ESU patch, flanked by two 'angry 8-balls', and the lettering: Anytime Baby, along with all ten trucks, the A-Team and WMD listed. The design features a cross cut border.

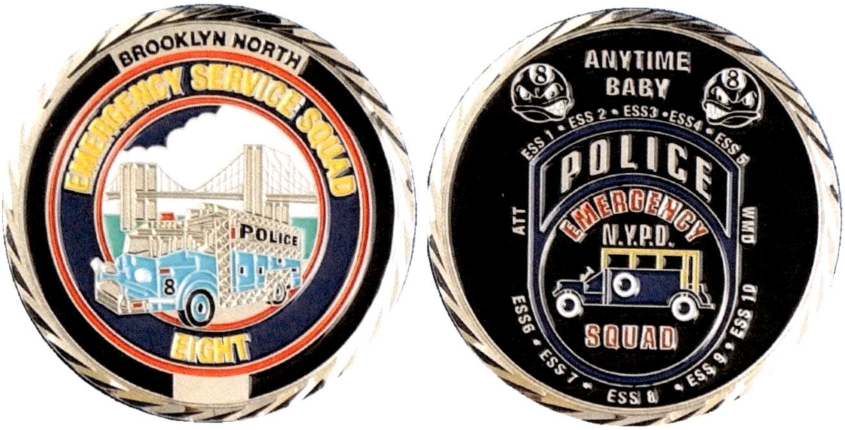

1st Issue coin

In 2016, Detective Michael Taggert had *All About Coins* produce the second Truck 8 challenge coin.

The 2" round, silver metal design featured the unit's 'angry 8-ball' logo on the obverse and the round ESU patch, on the reverse. The design features a cross cut border along with a small rectangular area under the ESU truck where it could be personalized.

2nd Issue - Silver coin

In addition, a limited edition, second run was done in gold and was made available only to ESU personnel. Unlike the silver coins, these gold coins were individually numbered.

2nd Issue - Gold coin (ESU members only)

TRUCK NINE (QUEENS)

In 2003, Detectives Andy Bershad and Todd Sessa designed the first Truck 9 challenge coin. The 1.75" round, antique silver metal coin was produced by *We Make Coins*. It features the ESU patch on the obverse, superimposed over an American flag with the lettering: Emergency Service Unit / Anytime, Anywhere. On the reverse is the NYPD patch with the lettering: Police Department – City of New York / NYPD ESU.

While it was created by Truck 9, it didn't specify any command designator, like the original Truck 6 coin, so that it could be used throughout ESU.

1st Issue coin

In 2014, Detectives Brian Brown and Mike O'Neill designed the second Truck 9 challenge coin. The 2" round, silver metal design was produced by *Signature Promotions*. The obverse side features the units white truck, superimposed over an NYPD patch, with the lettering: NYPD / Emergency Service Unit.

On the reverse is an armored Lenco Bearcat vehicle, superimposed over an ESU patch, with the lettering: Truck 9 / Queens.

2nd Issue coin

In addition, there was a *members only* version of the coin that was also produced. It maintained all of the same design elements, but was produced in gold.

2nd Issue - Members only coin (Photo courtesy of Mike O'Neill)

TRUCK TEN (QUEENS)

In 2011, Detective Rob Isernia had *Quality Challenge Coins* produce the first Truck 10 challenge coin. The 1.75" round, silver metal design featured the unit's old patch logo, a white ESU truck superimposed over the World's Fair Unisphere, with the lettering: Emergency Service / Squad 10 NYPD, on the obverse. The initials 'PT' and 'TL' on the border honor the two Truck 10 members, Police Officer's Paul Talty and Thomas Langone, who were killed in the September 11th terror attack.

On the reverse, is the ESU patch, superimposed over an American flag, with the lettering: Emergency Service / Squad 10, along the outside edge.

1st Issue coin

In 2014, Detective Isernia had *Adrenaline Challenge Coins* produce the second Truck 10 challenge coin. The 1.75" round, silver metal coin retained all the main elements of the previous design, but was updated to include the unit's new Mack-Saulsbury truck on the obverse.

The reverse side is the ESU patch superimposed over an American flag. The most significant change to the coin was the addition of a bezel cut border.

2nd Issue coin

SPECIALIZED UNITS

APPREHENSION & TACTICAL TEAM (A-TEAM)

The first A-Team challenge coin was produced in 2012, by Detective Thomas Longa and was made by *Coins Your Way*. The 1.5" high, silver metal coin is shaped like the unit's patch.

On the obverse is the unit's logo, a Spartan helmet with the legend: *Cohors Praetoria*, in Latin, which means: Praetorian Guard, along with the lettering: A-Team / VII IV / NYC. The exact meaning of the Roman numerals: VII and IV are known to the members of the unit.

On the reverse side is the unit's 4th issue patch which features a kneeling ESU operator, superimposed over an NYPD patch, and the lettering: A-Team / NYPD Emergency Service Unit / Apprehension Tactical Team. This coin featured a sand-blasted metal background.

1st Issue coin

In 2013, the second A-Team challenge coin was designed by Detective Longa and was produced by *Coins Your Way*. This coin featured the same design elements of the previous coin, but the silver metal coin was enlarged to 2" high and featured a black enamel background.

2nd Issue coin

The third A-Team challenge coin was designed in 2015, by Detective Longa and was again produced by *Coins Your Way*. The 2.5" high silver metal coin is in the shape of a body-bunker, a ballistic shield used by the unit during tactical entries.

On the obverse was the unit's Spartan helmet patch logo, with the lettering: City of New York Police Department / Emergency Service Unit / Apprehension Tactical Team.

The reverse side of the coin featured three of the unit's prior patch designs with the lettering: Holding the Standard / Since 1989.

3rd Issue coin

The fourth issue A-Team challenge coin was produced in 2016, by Detective Longa and was made by *Coins Your Way*.

The 2.5" high silver metal coin features the same Spartan helmet patch logo on the obverse with the addition of the date: 1989. On the reverse side is the teams 1st issue round patch, which shows two ESU operators and the lettering: Apprehension Tactical Team / NYPD / ESU. On the top is a tab with the lettering: A-Team.

4th Issue coin

CANINE TEAM

In 2015, Police Officer Benny Colecchia had *Challenge Coins Ltd.* produce the first Canine Team challenge coin. The 1.5" high, silver metal coin featured the unit's patch, a German shepherd with the lettering: Police / NYPD / ESU K-9 Team, on the obverse side. The reverse features a screen printed NYC skyline, with the WTC memorial blue lights. The coin has a clear epoxy cover on both sides.

1st Issue coin

In 2015, Officer Colecchia had *Challenge Coins Ltd.* produce the second Canine Team challenge coin. The size of the silver metal coin was increased to 2" high, and features the same design elements of the first coin; however, this version has a metal NYC skyline on the reverse, instead of the screen printed version, and does not have an epoxy cover.

2nd Issue coin

Later in 2015, another run of the 2nd issue coin was produced by Officer Colecchia. This design was the same as the previous version, but included a number and the lettering: *Canis Fidelis*, Latin for: Faithful Dog, along the edge of the coin.

In 2015, Tatyana Timoshenko, a civilian member of the Department and the mother of NYPD Detective Russell Timoshenko, who was shot in the line of duty and died on July 14th, 2007, produced a coin commemorating the naming of two canines in memory of her son.

The 2" round, gold coin features images of the two K9's and the patches for the NYPD and MTA, with the lettering: NYPD – K9 Timoshenko / MTA – K9 Shenko. There is also a motorcycle depicted, symbolizing Det. Timoshenko's love of motorcycles. On the reverse is a screen printed photo of the officer along with his name and his police officer and detective shield numbers in a banner.

Timoshenko Memorial K-9 coin

COUNTER SNIPER TEAM

I would be remiss if I didn't say this right up front about the Counter Sniper Team coin: *It is a riddle, wrapped in a mystery, inside an enigma.* Those who know how much effort that went into researching the history of this coin will understand and I beg forgiveness for the multitude of phone calls, texts and emails to all involved.

In approximately 2005, Detective Chuck King had *Northwest Territorial Mint* produce the first Counter Sniper Team challenge coin. The 1.75" round, antique silver metal coin featured the unit's logo, with the NYC Skyline in a cross-hair reticle, and the lettering: Long Range / NYPD / ESU / Counter Sniper Team, on the obverse. On the reverse side is an American flag and lettering: NYPD ESU / CST and the Latin phrase: *Firmitas Dignitas Virtus*, which, when translated, means: Tenacity, Dignity & Courage.

Rough art work-up (Photo courtesy of Chuck King)

In the original artwork, the flag on the reverse side was flat. After it went to graphic artist it was changed to a waving pattern.

Pre-Production Graphic (Photo courtesy of Chuck King)

Prior to production some minor changes were made to include black enamel in the scope sight on the obverse as well as black enamel in the lettering: NYPD ESU CST on the reverse side.

1st Issue coin

A few years later, a second run was produced by Detective Sean Mulcahy using a different company and mold. As a result, very minor differences can be found between the two. In addition to the silver version, a limited number of *members only* antique gold coins were also produced. These gold coins are individually numbered.

1st Issue Members Only coin (Photo courtesy of Chuck King)

In 2011, Detective Mulcahy had *Warrior Chips* produce the first Counter Sniper Team poker chip. The 1.75" round design features many of the key elements of the original metal coin, but the lettering "NYPD ESU CST" was removed from the flag side.

1st Issue 'Poker Chip'

A few years after the poker chip was produced, Detective Mulcahy produced a new CST coin. While the new coin maintained all the elements of the original, this version was produced in hard enamel, instead of the soft enamel that the original used.

2nd Issue coin

In 2016, Detective George Krant produced a reissue of the CST coin. While the new coin maintained all the elements of the 2nd issue coin, the overall size was increased to nearly 2" diameter and produced on a different mold. As a result, there are minor differences in the lettering and details.

3rd Issue coin (Photo courtesy Frank Ferrara)

EMERGENCY MEDICAL SQUAD

In 2015, Police Office John Ippolito had *Empire Coin* produce the first Emergency Medical Squad challenge coin.

1st Issue coin

The 2" round, silver metal design features a scalloped edge. On the obverse is a medical caduceus, with the NYPD flag in the background, and the lettering: Emergency / NYPD ESU / Medical Squad.

The reverse side features the Medical Squad's logo along with an ESU patch and the lettering: NYPD Emergency Service Unit / Emergency Medical Squad.

The Emergency Medical Squad is a unit within ESU that provides ambulance service for active and retired members of the NYPD of all ranks.

SPECIALIZED TRAINING SCHOOL

STS: *SCHOOL COIN*

In 2016, Sgt. John Flynn designed the first ESU Specialized Training School challenge coin. The 1.75" round, antique silver design features several of the components of ESU training: Body Bunker, flanked by an H&K MP5 & M-4 rifle, Hazmat placard, Medical Caduceus, Rappel Carabineer, Jaws of Life, and PADI diver flag. Along the border is the lettering: Specialized Training School / *In Omnia Paratus*, Latin for: Ready for Anything.

On the reverse side is the ESU logo, superimposed over crossed U.S. and NYPD flags and the date 1930. Along the border is the lettering: NYPD Emergency Service Unit / Anytime, Anywhere.

Specialized Training School coin

STS: *EMT COIN*

In 2015, Detectives Andy Bershad and Dennis Cannale designed and produced the first Emergency Medical Technician School coin. The 1.75" round, antique silver design was produced by *All About Coins.*

On the obverse is the ESU logo in the center with the lettering: Emergency Medical Training School / Emergency Service Unit. On the reverse are two crossed M-4's, superimposed over an American flag, and a medical caduceus. Along the border is the lettering: Good Medicine in Bad Places / *Ut Ceteri Vivant*, Latin for: So That Others May Live.

Emergency Medical Training School coin

STS: *CLASS COINS*

In 1999, a coin was issued to the STS class according to one of the graduates. It is similar in design to the one done by Truck 6. The round, antique silver metal, challenge coin is approximately 1.5" and features all the same elements of the Truck 6 coin, but with a slightly different color scheme on the obverse (Tomcat) side.

It should be noted that the one depicted below is the actual one given out to the class. Over the years I have seen several others surface, but these have all had minor variations and are not the STS class version.

1999 STS coin (Photo courtesy Anthony Lisi)

In 2010, Detective Ryan Norman designed and produced this STS class coin for Group 3. The 1.75", silver metal coin was produced by *All About Coins*. The obverse features an ESU patch in the center with the 10 ESU trucks written around it. On the outer border is the lettering: STS 2010 / Group 3. Above the ESU logo is a rectangular metal box where each coin was numbered.

On the reverse side is a Tomcat, holding an American flag, leaning on an ESU patch with the lettering: Thank God / You're Here.

2010 STS coin (Photo courtesy of Ryan Norman)

In 2015, Sergeant Matt Zucker, along with Lieutenant Keith Humm, had *Coins for Anything* produce a 2" round, antique silver challenge coin for their STS class, which was presented to both the instructors and students.

In coming up with the conceptual design of the STS coin, Sgt. Zucker wanted to incorporate an image which he had seen on the coin produced for Medal of Honor recipient, Lieutenant Michael P. Murphy, a U.S. Navy SEAL who was killed in Afghanistan on June 28th, 2005, during Operation Red Wings. That particular design featured a 3-D image of Lt. Murphy, holding his M4, superimposed over a map of Afghanistan along with his MOH and SEAL trident.

The first iteration of the artwork featured an ESU patch in the center of the obverse with the lettering: Specialized Training School / 2015. On the reverse is an ESU operator, surrounded by a pair of SCUBA fins, Tactical Medic logo, WMD logo and an operator rappelling down a rope line, with the NYPD motto: Fidelis Ad Mortem. The interior of the ESU patch was originally going to have a sandblasted finish.

Proposed artwork for STS 2015 coin – 1st Version (Courtesy of Matt Zucker)

The second design added black enamel to the ESU patch along with different icons for the Rappelling and SCUBA components.

Proposed artwork for STS 2015 coin – 2nd Version (Courtesy of Matt Zucker)

The 2nd version obverse design, featuring the black enamel inside the ESU patch, was approved. Although the ESU operator was kept on the reverse, small changes were made to the positioning of the training icons representing the various components of ESU school training: Rappelling, Scuba, WMD's and Tactical Medicine. Also added to the background was the image of Molly the cow, the unofficial mascot of ESU.

In addition, the NYPD motto was removed and the names of the agencies participating in the training: NYPD, PAPD (Port Authority Police Dept.), JCPD (Jersey City Police Dept.) and NYCD (New York City Corrections Dept.), along with the inscription: *Viam Inveniemus*, Latin for: We Will Find A Way, was added.

2015 STS coin (Photo courtesy of Matt Zucker)

TACTICAL MEDIC

In 2007, Detective Shawn Soler designed and produced the first Tactical Medic challenge coin.

The 2" round, gold metal coin features the unit's logo on the obverse side, a modified medical Star of Life logo with yellow EKG rhythm, and the lettering: Tactical / NYPD / Medic. Along the border is the motto: *Medicina Bona Locis Malis*, Latin for: Good Medicine in Bad Places. On the reverse side is a modified caduceus symbol that features a dagger, two intertwined snakes, a pair of wings and the lettering: Tactical / NYPD / Medic.

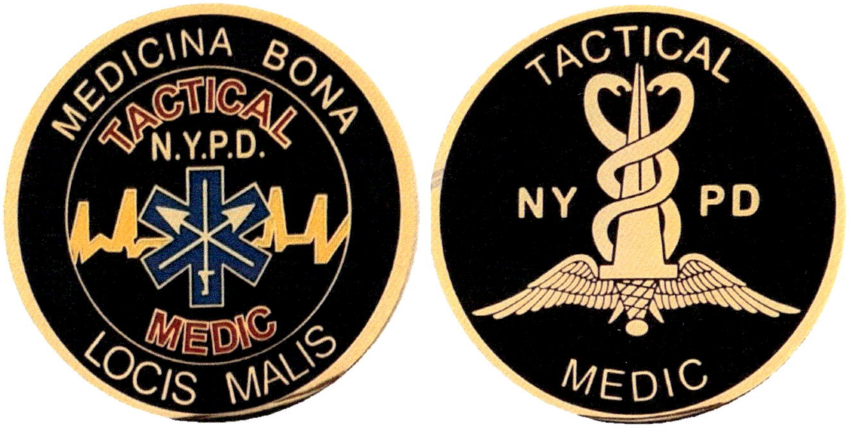

1st Issue coin

WATER RESCUE

In 2015, Detectives Donald LaSala and David Norman had *NG Slater Co.* produce the first Water Rescue Squad challenge coin.

The 2" round, silver metal design featured a Tomcat, standing on a dock, wearing SCUBA gear and holding a PADI flag with the legend: Emergency Service / NYPD Water Rescue. On the reverse is a PADI flag with an ESU patch superimposed over it with the admonition: Never Forget.

1st Issue coin

WEAPONS OF MASS DESTRUCTION TEAM

In 2006, Detective Patrick Barry had *We Make Coins* produce the first Weapons of Mass Destruction Team challenge coins.

The 1.75" round, silver coins featured various CBRNE (Chemical, Biological, Radiological, Nuclear, & Explosives) icons on the obverse with the lettering: Weapons of Mass Destruction / Response Team. On the reverse side is the ESU '23' patch logo, superimposed over an American flag, with the lettering: NYPD / Emergency Service Unit.

1st Issue coin

In 2011, Detective Armando Droz produced the second Weapons of Mass Destruction Team challenge coin. The 1.5" round, silver coin featured a skull with gas mask on the obverse, superimposed over a biohazard icon, with the lettering: Weapons of Mass Destruction / NYC.

On the reverse is the ESU patch with the lettering: City of New York / Emergency Service Unit. The background, on each side of the coin, was done in a diamond plate design and the lettering and eyes, on the obverse side, was done in a glow-in-the-dark paint.

2nd Issue coin

In 2013, Detective Droz produced the third Weapons of Mass Destruction Team challenge coin. The silver coin featured all the same design elements as the previous version, but the size was enlarged to 2" diameter.

3rd Issue coin

EVENTS & *MISCELLANEOUS*

9/11 TERROR ATTACK

In October of 2001, Police Officer Rick Martinez of Truck 3 had *Corporate Gifts Unlimited* produce a challenge coin to recognize the members of the Emergency Service Unit who were lost in the September 11th attack.

The 2" round, antique gold metal coin featured the NYPD logo, NYC skyline, and the lettering: NYPD Emergency Service Unit on the obverse. Along the outer border is the lettering: Forever in Our Hearts, as well as fourteen stars, symbolizing each of the ESU officers who died on September 11th.

On the reverse is the ESU patch, in the center of the coin, surrounded by the names of the fallen and the lettering: September 11th, 2011 and the NYPD motto. The fourteen stars are also replicated on the border.

Forever In Our Hearts 9/11 Memorial Coin

In 2005, Detectives David Norman and Donald LaSala designed and produced a 1.75" round, gold metal challenge coin to commemorate the 10th anniversary of the September 11th attack and the ensuing *War on Terror*. The obverse features the Twin Towers in the center, surrounded by 14 gold stars, honoring the ESU officers lost in the initial attack, and the lettering: War on Terror / Never Forget / September 11th, 2001 – September 11th, 2011.

The reverse side features the 1930's green Mack truck with the lettering: Emergency / NYPD / Squad. Along the outer border is the lettering: Police Department City of New York / Anything Anywhere Anytime. This coin has a clear epoxy cover.

War on Terror Anniversary Coin (Photo courtesy of Mike Dazi)

In 2016, NYPD Finest Lacrosse Team members, Detective Mike Riso and Sergeant Ted Jeremenko, designed a memorial coin honoring former team members, Detective Joe Vigiano and Police Officer Ronald Kloepfer, who were both killed in the September 11th terrorist attack. Officer Kloepfer had founded the Lacrosse team in 1993.

The 2" round, silver coin was produced by *Challenge Coins Ltd.* and features a clear epoxy cover, diamond cut border, along with gold accents and lettering. On the obverse is the NYC skyline with a Lacrosse helmet flanked on either side by the American and NYPD flags. On the bottom are two crossed Lacrosse sticks with the date: Est. 1993. The border features the lettering: Finest Lacrosse / New York City Police Department.

On the reverse side is a subdued American flag with a thin blue line through the center. The officer's shields and an ESU patch are featured in the center. Just above the badges are angel wings with RK7 and JV21, denoting the officers initials and their jersey numbers. Along the border is the lettering: Ronald Kloepfer & Joseph Vigiano / End of Watch 9-11-2001.

Lacrosse Team Memorial Coin

In 2016, retired NYPD Police Officer Kathy Vigiano, the widow of Detective Joe Vigiano, ESU Truck 2, and the couple's sons: Joe, Jim and John, collaborated on a challenge coin design. The coin commemorates the 15th anniversary of the annual Vigiano Brothers Memorial Ski Outing.

Vigiano Ski Trip Coin Original artwork (Courtesy of Kathy Vigiano)

The ski event honors the memory of Detective Vigiano and his brother, FDNY Firefighter John T. Vigiano II, who were both killed in the September 11th terrorist attack. The funds raised benefit the NYPD's Police Self Support Group and the Pre-1971 Firefighter Retirees (Lost Battalion). The coin was based on a design previously used on the memorial shirts.

The obverse features the Twin Towers, superimposed over an American flag, along with a shotgun and a Halligan tool and the two brother's respective NYPD and FDNY shields. Along the outer border are their names: Det. Joseph Vincent Vigiano / Fire Fighter John Thomas Vigiano II. The inclusion of the shotgun and Halligan tool is reminiscent of a famous photo taken of Joe and John, in their uniforms, in which Joe is holding the Halligan tool and John is holding the shotgun, swapping their respective 'tools of the trade,' so to speak.

On the reverse side is a modified version of the ESU Truck 2 Tomcat logo, along with the Ladder 132 flaming skull logo, on a red background. On the border is the lettering: NYPD Emergency Services Unit Truck 2 / FDNY Ladder Company 132. The 2" round, gold metal coin was produced in two variations. The first followed the original artwork, with a red enamel background, on the reverse side.

Red background version

A second coin was also produced and this featured a gold sandblasted background on the reverse side. Both styles were available for the memorial ski outing.

Gold background version

ESU ANNIVERSARY

In 2005, Detectives David Norman and Donald LaSala designed and produced a 1.75" round, gold metal challenge coin to commemorate the 75th anniversary of ESU. This coin has a clear epoxy cover.

The obverse featured the number: 75 and the lettering: Years of Service / 1930-2005, superimposed over an American flag. Along the outer border is the lettering: Preparedness is our Watchword / A Tradition of Excellence.

The reverse side features the 1930's green Mack truck with the lettering: Emergency / NYPD / Squad. Along the outer border is the lettering: Police Department City of New York / Anything Anywhere Anytime.

75th Anniversary Coin

In 2015, Detective Dennis Cannale had *All About Coins* produce a 2" round, silver metal challenge coin to commemorate the 85th anniversary of ESU.

The obverse features a white ESU truck, superimposed over an American flag, with a Tomcat leaning on the lettering: 85th Anniversary. Around the outer border is the lettering: Emergency Service Unit / Anything Anywhere Anytime and the dates: 1930 / 2015.

The reverse side features the 1930's green Mack truck superimposed over a black NYC skyline with the lettering: NYPD / Emergency Squad. Along the outer border is the lettering: Preparedness Remains Our Watchword / Est. April 10, 1930

85th Anniversary Coin

GENERIC

In the late 1990's, Tony Michalek designed and produced a 1.75" round, antique gold metal challenge coin. The obverse of the coin features an ESU patch with the lettering: Once An E-Man / April 10, 1930 / Always An E-Man.

In the center of the reverse side is the lettering: Emergency Service Unit / Truck 911 / For Those That Passed Before Us / REMA / For Those That Have Retired / NYPD. On the outer border is a listing of all the units within ESU.

All Metal version

In addition, a limited edition second version was also produced. This version retained all the elements of the previous design, but featured blue enamel within the ESU patch

Blue enamel version

Around 2010, Detective Sean Mulcahy had *Northwest Territorial Mint* produce a 1 5/8" round, antique silver metal challenge coin.

The obverse features the *new & old* Tomcat patch design. In the center, superimposed over an American flag, are two Tomcats, one wearing a ballistic helmet, tactical vest and M-4 and one wearing an old reefer coat, 8-point hat and holding a tommy gun, representing the current and past ESU officers, leaning on an ESU patch with the lettering: Est 1930. On the border is the lettering: NYPD / Emergency Service Unit.

In the center of the reverse side are the ESU and NYPD patches, in bare metal, along with a small box which could be used to personalize the coins.

Tomcats – metal version

In 2011, Detective Sean Mulcahy had *Warrior Chips* produce a 1.75" round, silver poker chip. The obverse featured the twin tomcat patch design, superimposed over an American flag, and the lettering NYPD Emergency Service Unit.

The reverse side was similar to the obverse, with the exception that the Tomcats were superimposed over a grey colored NYC skyline and American flag.

Tomcats – Poker Chip version

MSGT MCENIRY / USMC

In 2010, Detective James McEniry had *Honor Coins* produce a 2” round, gold sandblasted metal coin commemorating his service with both the Emergency Service Unit and the United States Marine Corps.

The obverse features the chevrons for his USMC rank of Master Gunnery Sergeant and the lettering: MGYSGT James McEniry / Semper Fi. The reverse features the traditional ESU round patch design in the center with the lettering: New York City Police Department / ESU.

MGYSGT McEniry coin

OPERATION HERCULES

In 2015, Detective Shawn Soler designed and produced the Operation Hercules challenge coin. The 1.75” round, antique silver design features an ESU officer, superimposed over the NYC skyline, with the lettering: NYPD ESU / Operation Hercules on the obverse.

On the reverse side it features the heads of a lion and bull, facing each other, with crossed swords in the middle and the lettering: *A true hero isn't measured by the size of his strength, but by the strength of his heart.*

Operation Hercules coin - Silver Version

A limited edition second version was also done in gold. These coins are numbered.

Operation Hercules coin - Gold Version

OPERATION TORCH

In 2015, Detective Shawn Soler also designed and produced the Operation Torch (**T**ransit **O**perational **R**esponse with **C**anine & **H**eavy weapons) challenge coin.

The 1.75" round, silver design featured an ESU officer and the Statue of Liberty, superimposed over the NYC skyline, with the lettering: NYPD ESU / Operation Torch, on the obverse.

The reverse side features a map of NYC with the routes of the Transit System in black enamel and the lettering: New York City / Transit Operational Response with Canine & Heavy Weapons.

Operation TORCH coin

RETIRED E-MAN ASSOCIATION (REMA)

In 2008, Officer Peter Knudsen, a member of the Suffolk County Police Department, designed and produced the first REMA coin for retired NYPD ESU officer, Tony Sanpietro. According to Knudsen, the original coin was produced by *eMILITARYcoins*, but later issued coins were produced by *Symbol Arts*.

The 1.75" round, gold coin features a rope border design. On the obverse side is an eagle, clutching an American flag, with the REMA logo. Along the outer border is the lettering: Retired Emergency Man's Association. Just above the eagle's wings is a small banner where the coin could be personalized.

On the reverse side are the NYPD and ESU patches, superimposed over an NYPD flag, and the lettering: REMA Jul 26, 1996 / NYPD Jul 1845 / ESU Apr 10, 1930. Beneath the patches is the NYPD motto: Fidelis Ad Mortem.

REMA coin (Official)

During the original design phase he received input from Tony Sanpietro, as well as retired Lieutenant Al Baker, regarding the different elements they wanted to include. Tony had insisted on the eagle, signifying the strength of the United States, and Al wanted the rope border included as an *homage* to the unit's foundation in rescue work.

On a historical note, Knudsen's father, Richard, and his grandfather, Peter, were both members of the NYPD ESU. Sadly, his grandfather was killed in the line of duty on November 25th, 1946, when he and his partner, Patrolman Francis O'Hara, were attempting to cut off a gas leak.

The two men had entered the basement of a building when an explosion occurred and the officers were killed instantly. ESU Lieutenant Charles Michie attempted to rescue the patrolmen, but exerted himself to such an extent that he collapsed amid the debris and died. Prior to the September 11th, 2001 terror attack, it had been the deadliest day within the ESU family.

In 2015, another REMA challenge coin was designed and produced by Tony Agugliaro, a retired member of ESU. The 2" round, silver coin was produced by *Coins Your Way* and was intended to be an update to the original REMA coin. However, this particular coin was not officially sanctioned by the organization.

On the obverse is the REMA logo, superimposed over an American flag, with the lettering: Emergency Service Unit / Anytime Anywhere. Under the patch is a small rectangular box where these coins were numbered.

On the reverse is the 'Retired, Baby....!' patch logo, a Tomcat in a Hawaiian shirt, holding a Pina Colada and smoking a cigar, which was produced by *Huntzman Enterprises* in 2009. On the outer border is the lettering: Emergency Service Unit / Retired, Baby....!

REMA coin (Unofficial)

NYC HOUSING & TRANSIT COINS

In 2014, two commemorative coins were produced to recognize the pre-merger Emergency Rescue Units of the Housing and Transit Police Departments. Neither of these coins were an official issue, as each unit had ceased to exist as an independent entity in 1995.

HAPD – EMERGENCY RESCUE

This 2" round, gold metal coin features a modified version of the unit's patch, the New York City skyline, with the Twin Towers, and a medical Star of Life symbol, and the lettering: Housing Police / Emergency Rescue / New York City, in the center of the obverse side.

The reverse features the HAPD patch, superimposed over the American flag, and lettering: New York City Housing Authority Police Department / 1952-1995.

The lettering: Second to None, is repeated along the outer border on each side.

HAPD – Emergency Rescue coin

TAPD – EMERGENCY MEDICAL RESCUE

This 2" round, gold metal coin features a diamond cut border. In the center of the obverse side is the Warner Brothers cartoon character, Taz, the unofficial mascot of the unit, standing on a set of railroad tracks and holding a subway car above his head. Around his neck is an H&K MP5 and leaning up against him are the Jaws of Life. Along the border is the lettering: Emergency Rescue / Transit Police.

The reverse side features the TAPD patch, superimposed over the American flag, and the lettering: New York City Transit Police Department / 1953-1995.

TAPD – Emergency Rescue coin

It should be noted that the designer(s) of these two coins incorrectly made the background of both the HAPD and TAPD patches black enamel, instead of the correct Navy blue.

UNKNOWN

During my research I identified a number of coins which could not be attributed to a particular officer or truck. I have included these and once again ask for any help in determining the authenticity of these items. The following coins were all produced after the September 11th terror attack. I believe that these coins were sanctioned ESU coins, but unfortunately my research has failed to identity those involved in the production of these coins.

The first coin is approximately 1.5" round, silver metal, multi-agency coin. The obverse features an NYPD police officer's shield with the numbers 0911 in the number panel. Along the border are the agency names: NYPD ESU / PAPD ESU / NYSP MRT (Mobile Response Team) & NYDOC ESU.

On the reverse side is a depiction of the façade of the World Trade Center with the lettering: 09/11/01 – World Trade Center Rescue and Recovery Operation.

9/11 – Rescue & Recovery coin

The second is a slightly smaller than 1.75" round, silver metal coin. The obverse features the ESU patch with the lettering: We Will Never Forget / 9-11-01.

On the reverse side is a depiction of the Twin Towers and Pentagon, superimposed over an American flag, with the lettering: God May Have Mercy on You, We Will Not – September 11, 2001.

9/11 – We Will Never Forget coin

The third coin is an approximately 1.75" round, silver metal coin. The obverse features the ESU '23' patch logo in the center, superimposed over an NYPD flag, with the lettering: Emergency Service Unit. On the reverse is the NYPD patch, superimposed over an American Flag, with the lettering: New York City Police Department.

9/11 – '23' coin

REPRODUCTIONS

In my first book, I said that I would have been remiss if I didn't address the issue of reproductions, as it was one of the driving forces for writing the original insignia book. I would like to say that this isn't the case with coins, but that would be a lie.

Because of the popularity of NYPD coins it was only a matter of time before reproductions would begin to surface. Many of us wanted to believe that the initial outlay, coupled with the mold charges, would prevent reproductions, but we were wrong. When you see coins routinely selling for $100, $200 and more, it is obvious that such high demand will offset any start-up costs.

While the majority of the ESU coins have only been around for a handful of years, there are still several that are much older and quite rare. It is not unusual then that the purveyors of fake / reproduction coins would jump on the bandwagon and produce knockoffs to sell to unsuspecting collectors.

It was my hope that in writing this book I could educate collectors about some of the history and details that could help them navigate the rocky shoals of coin collecting.

As of this writing I know of at least one confirmed reproduction of the 2nd issue A-Team coin as well as several others that I consider rather questionable. I had thought about including them, but I didn't want to tip them off to the mistake and have them correct it.

The best advice I can give to collectors, who wish to avoid these pitfalls, is to make sure that you obtain the items from reputable sources. In the military collecting community there is an old adage that rings true in the law enforcement field as well: *Buy the item, not the story.*

At the end of the day, asking questions, independent research and trusted sources are still your best bet to avoid getting burned.

ADDENDUM

"*You're never done and you never stop learning.*"

The field of collecting and researching ESU insignia is a continually evolving one. Each year new insignia is released, while other, previously unknown, ones are discovered.

One of the most frustrating things for me, as a researcher and author, is to have to grudgingly accept the fact that some information will remain elusive, at least for the time being. In reading this book you will have undoubtedly noticed that some items are clearly attributed, while others are a bit more *vague*. The reason for this is that, while I may *know* that a particular item was done by a certain officer or produced at a certain period of time, I have been hesitant to add this information without actual corroboration. I think it would be grossly unfair for me to identify someone and then have to do a retraction later. Any new information that is uncovered will be added to future editions.

For those of you who know of any ESU items that should be included, or who have information that would aid to the accuracy of this book, I ask that you please contact me. I am also interested in any personal photos showing officers wearing insignia as well as old NYPD, HAPD or TAPD ESU vehicles.

You can find information on how to reach me on my author page at the end of this book.

About the Author

Andrew G. Nelson is a twenty-two year law enforcement veteran and a graduate of the State University of New York. He served twenty years with the New York City Police Department, achieving the rank of sergeant before retiring in 2005.

He is the author of several fiction novels as well as non-fiction books on the New York City Police Department's Emergency Service Unit.

He and his wife have four children and reside with their Irish Wolfhound in central Illinois.

For more information please visit:

http://andrewgnelson.blogspot.com/

Like us on Facebook:

https://www.facebook.com/pages/Andrew-Nelson/168310343376572

NYPD

Made in United States
Orlando, FL
11 May 2026

81389044R00071